Fr. Benjamin Sember

Twelve Lessons on the Catholic Faith

Twelve Lessons on the Catholic Faith
Fr. Benjamin Sember

Copyright ©2012, Fr. Benjamin Sember All rights reserved

Cover image: Brian Buettner
Cover and book design: Tau Publishing Design Department

The *Imprimatur* granted on September 14, 2012 by The Most Reverend David L. Ricken, DD, JCL Bishop of Green Bay.

The *Nihil Obstat* granted on September 14, 2012 by Reverend Alfred McBride, O. Praem.

No part of this book may be reproduced, stored in a retrieval system or transmitted in any form or by any means - electronic, mechanical, photocopying, recording, or otherwise - without written permission of the publisher.

For information regarding permission, write to:
Tau Publishing, LLC
Attention: Permissions Dept.
4727 North 12th street
Phoenix, AZ 85014

ISBN 978-1-61956-026-0

First Edition September 2012
10 9 8 7 6 5 4 3 2 1

Published and printed in the United States of America by Tau Publishing, LLC
For additional inspirational books visit us at Tau-Publishing.com

Tau-Publishing.com
Words of Inspiration

Dear Marjie,
May God bless you and those you love. In Christ,
Fr Benjamin

Dedicated to the
Queen of Heaven,
Our Lady of Good Help

Index

Introduction	1
Lesson 1: **God Created the Whole World**	3
Lesson 2: **God's Plan of Love**	7
Lesson 3: **God Makes a Covenant**	11
Lesson 4: **God Sends a Savior**	19
Lesson 5: **The Trinity and Jesus Christ**	27
Lesson 6: **The Church is the Family of God**	33
Lesson 7: **The Seven Sacraments**	39
Lesson 8: **Doing Good and Avoiding Evil**	47
Lesson 9: **Prayer is Being with God**	53
Lesson 10: **Mary and the Saints**	57
Lesson 11: **Angels**	63
Lesson 12: **The Resurrection and Life Everlasting**	67
List of Questions for Memorization	71

Introduction

These Twelve Lessons are designed to give an introduction to the Catholic faith which is simple and clear, but at the same time thorough and rich with details. These lessons are written so that parents can read them to their children. The important points are brought within the reach of a child, but without taking away their robust and authentic character. Many of the details are left out so that the main points and the overall direction of the stories is obvious. For this reason it is important to use Bible stories and prayer books to supplement the lessons.

The lessons will be more effective if parents read each lesson at least twice before moving on to the next one, because children enjoy repetition and they will absorb more from each lesson as they become comfortable with it. The lessons are very full, and parents should feel free to pause for conversation, and even stop at a natural break and continue the lesson later. The questions at the end of the lesson are not a quiz; they are a way of presenting the main points in a form that is simple and easy to remember. The questions in *italics* could be memorized by children who are preparing to receive their First Communion. Also, it is possible to read Lesson 8 immediately after Lesson 2 in preparation for the sacrament of Confession.

These lessons are also an excellent resource for teenagers and adults who need a simple guide to the Catholic faith. Teens and adults should have their own copy of the Bible at hand, as well as a catechism that will be able to answer their questions. Above all, a good Catholic is the best guide a person can have to the faith. This is because Christianity is not essentially something you learn, but something you live. No one can claim to know the Christian faith unless he has been carrying his own cross and following Jesus every day (Luke 9:23).

Jesus is our master and teacher, and by the power of the

Resurrection He walks with His disciples, especially through the gift of the Eucharist. The Eucharist is the greatest treasure our Church carries on her journey through history. The saints who have gone before us, who now live in glory with God, are also great treasures and wonderful friends. The lives of the saints give us real examples of what the faith looks like when it is lived to a heroic degree, and so the lives of the saints should be part of any introduction to Catholicism.

The first among the saints is the Blessed Virgin Mary, who was the first disciple of Jesus, and who followed Him faithfully all the way to the cross (John 19:25-27). Since Mary has an important role in our salvation, she is also given an important place is these lessons.

When the Blessed Virgin Mary appeared in Wisconsin in 1859, she told a young woman, "Gather the children in this wild country and teach them what they should know for salvation." The woman, Adele Brise, responded, "How shall I teach them who know so little myself?" These lessons are dedicated to the Queen of Heaven, Our Lady of Good Help, who promised, "Go and fear nothing. I will help you." Adele Brise was 28 years old at the time, and she spent the rest of her life teaching the Catholic faith.

Fr. Benjamin Sember

Lesson 1

God Created the Whole World

Before the world was made, God existed. God always has been, and God always will be. We say that God is *eternal*, which means that He has no beginning and no end. We say that God is a mystery, because He is more than our minds can understand. We also say that God is the Holy Trinity, because He is one God in three persons. The three persons in God are the Father, the Son, and the Holy Spirit. Even though there are three persons in God, there is only one God. There is a perfect unity in God, and God is perfect love.

God created the whole world because He wanted to share His goodness and His love. The Bible tells us that God created with His Word, which means that when God said something, that thing began to exist. The Word of God is another name for the Son of God, and through Him all things were made. God the Father made everything through the Son, in the power of the Holy Spirit.

When God said, "Let there be light," suddenly there was light. God saw that the light was good, and He divided the light from the darkness. God formed all the stars, making some of them big and bright, and some of them little and dim. He arranged the stars into galaxies, and He created comets and asteroids. God gave a few of the stars planets to orbit around them, and a few of the planets had little moons to keep them company. Some of the planets were big, like Jupiter, and some of them were very small, like Pluto. One of the planets God made was not very big, but it had something special: this planet was filled with water. God called the water "the sea," and He made boundaries for the sea so that it would not cover the whole planet, but instead there would be dry places called "the land." God formed the mountains, and the hills and the valleys.

Then God made life on the planet. He made plants to cover the land, like grasses and flowers and bushes and trees. Each plant was given a special way to reproduce itself by making little seeds. Seeds have the power to grow into new plants so that there will always be plants. Some plants hide their seeds in things that we can eat, like fruits and vegetables and berries.

God also made plants that grow in the sea, like algae and seaweed. He made fish to swim in the sea, and all sorts of other swimming things like corals and jellyfish and shrimp. God filled the oceans and the seas with all kinds of swimming animals. God also make swimming things for the rivers and the lakes.

Then God made birds to fill the sky. He made tiny hummingbirds, and hawks and eagles and penguins. God gave the birds feathers and wings, and He gave some of them beautiful voices, so that they could chirp, and twitter, and sing. God also made insects and spiders, worms and lizards, and all kinds of butterflies. God made strange and wonderful animals, and God saw that they were good.

Then God made mammals, and He gave them the ability to make milk so they could nurse their babies, which none of the other animals can do. God made the squirrels and the chipmunks, He made the deer and the beavers, He made elephants and tigers, and He made flying bats. God even made mammals that swim in the sea, like dolphins and whales.

Every animal that God made was wonderful and perfect in its own way, and God saw that it was good. God gave each animal everything that it would need to find food, to make a nest or a den or a hole in the ground, and to have babies and raise them. God even made animals that no one has ever seen, because they became extinct long ago or because they have not yet been discovered.

God created all these wonderful animals, but God was not finished with His work. God had one more creature to make that would be more wonderful than anything He had created on the earth. The last creature God made was man. God made man in His image and likeness, meaning that human beings are more like God than any other creature God created on the earth. The special gift that God gave human beings is called the *soul*, and human beings are the only creatures that are made of a body and a soul. The soul allows us to think, and to choose, and to love. People are the only living things that can have a conversation, and plan what they are going to do tomorrow, and fall in love, and get married, and send invitations to their wedding.

God made human beings to be His friends on earth, and to care for all of creation. We can care for the plants by giving them what they need to grow, and by pruning them, and giving them water when they are thirsty. We can care for the animals by making sure that they have a place to live and food to eat. We can also create new things. Many of the things that we see in the world were invented by people. The buildings, the roads, the boats and all kinds of machines were made by human beings. People invented a way to write, and people invented books to read, and we can do all these things because God made us in His image and likeness. God is a creator, and God gave us some of His power so that we can create things too.

There is an even more amazing way that we share in God's work, because we can help God to create new people. God did not make everyone right away, but He started with just one man and one woman. The man's name was Adam, and the woman's name was Eve. God made a man and a woman so that they could be friends and love one another. God blessed them with a special gift, called *fertility*, so that they could get married and start a family. Adam and Eve gave the gift of life to their children, and their children got married and had more children, and so every person on earth came from the same very-great-grandfather and the same very-great-grandmother. We are all part of one very big family.

This is how God gave the gift of life to you. Your life came from God, through Adam and Eve, and through your mother and your father. At the moment of conception you began to exist in your mother's womb as one tiny cell, and God gave you a soul so that you would be able to think, to choose, and to love. God also formed your body and all its parts. God makes each person special and unique, and He gives gifts to some people that He does not give to other people. Even when God makes identical twins, He forms one a little differently from the other, because God never makes the same person twice. God loves you with a special love that is different from the way that God loves anyone else. You are very precious, because there will never be another person just like you. God is love, and when God looks at you, He sees that you are very good, and He loves you very much.

Lesson 1:
God Created the Whole World

1. ***Where did the world come from?***
   God created the whole world out of nothing.

2. Why did God create the world?
   God created the world to share His goodness and His love.

3. Where did God come from?
   God always has been and always will be.

4. What does it mean to say that God is eternal?
   Eternal means that God has no beginning and no end.

5. Why do we say that God is love?
   We say that God is love because the Father, the Son, and the Holy Spirit are united in perfect love.

6. Who were the first human beings?
   The first human beings were a man named Adam and a woman named Eve.

7. What is special about human beings?
   Human beings are made of body and soul, created in the image and likeness of God.

8. What does the soul allow a person to do?
   The soul allows a person to think, to choose, and to love.

9. ***Who made you?***
   God made me.

10. How did God make you?
    God gave me the gift of life through my father and mother, and He formed me in my mother's womb.

Lesson 2

God's Plan of Love

In the beginning, God created the world and all the living creatures. God is love, and He created everything because He wanted to share His goodness and His love. God gives a little bit of His goodness to each of the things that He creates, and so everything God makes is good. Even though God has created so many things, God is still greater than all the things that He has made. This is why we say that God is a mystery, because He is more than our minds can understand.

God wanted to share His love, and so He created human beings in His image and likeness. He gave us the gift of a soul, so that we would be able to think, to choose, and to love. God is love, and He created us to live in His love and to love one another, and to help care for the beautiful world.

God made one man, named Adam, and one woman, named Eve. He made a garden named Eden for them to live in, and He filled the garden with plants and animals. All the different plants and all the wonderful animals would show Adam and Eve how good God is, and how wise God is, and how much He loved them. God would come and talk to them every day, and Adam and Eve were friends with God.

They had the freedom to make choices, and so God gave them different choices to make. He made many trees with different kinds of fruit, and they could eat whatever fruit they wanted. God gave Adam and Eve one commandment: He told them not to eat from the tree in the center of the garden. They were free to eat from every other tree, but not from that one.

Adam and Eve began to explore their new home, and Eve went over to look at the tree that grew in the center of the garden. She noticed that the fruit *looked* like it was tasty and good to eat. There was also a serpent there, who told Eve that if she ate from that tree, she would become like God, knowing good and evil. Eve did not know what evil was, because everything God had made was good. Eve took some of the fruit, and she gave some to her husband, and they both ate it.

This was a sin! They did not trust God, and they did not listen to Him, and so they brought evil into the world for the first time. Because of their sin, they lost their friendship with God and became filled with fear and guilt. They lost their special friendship with each other, which means that they would begin to argue and fight. They also lost their home in the Garden of Eden, and they had to go and find a new home outside, where they would suffer and work for their food.

The sin of Adam and Eve is called *original sin*, because it was the first bad thing that was done on earth. Each of the children of Adam and Eve, and all their grandchildren, and every human being after them, was born with this burden called original sin. *Original sin* means that it is not easy for us to trust in God. It also means that we need to work very hard not to be selfish. *Selfish* means that people care more for themselves than for other people. They try to take the best for themselves, by tricking other people or by stealing from them, or by making laws that are unfair. Instead of a world filled with love, sin makes a world filled with anger and fear. Sin has caused all the sadness in the world.

Not only did people become selfish and begin to argue and fight, but they did not trust God and they were not friends with God. People ignored God or they were afraid of Him. Some people said that, because they could not see God, God did not exist. Some people worshiped the sun because it was so bright and its light was so strong that they thought it must be a god. Other people worshiped the moon, or mountains, or rivers. Some people invented strange gods. They took a piece of wood or stone, and carved it so that it would have eyes and a mouth and a nose. Then they gave it a strange name, and made it an idol. Whenever they wanted a blessing, they would bring a present to their idol and ask for help. When God did anything good for these people, they would thank their idol, because they did not understand that all blessings come from God. God wanted to free people from their strange gods, but the more God blessed them, the more they became confused.

Of course, God was not surprised that things happened this

way, because God knows everything. He knew that when He gave human beings the freedom to serve Him, we would also be free to reject Him. God knew that when He gave us the power to love, we could also choose not to love. God knew what bad things we could do, but God still loved the people He had made, and He had a plan to save us from our sins. God promised Adam and Eve that one day He would send a Savior. In the next lesson, we will find out how God prepared the world to receive a Savior, because it took centuries and centuries to make everything ready for Him to come.

Lesson 2:
God's Plan of Love

11. **Why did God make us?**
    God is love, and He made us to live in His love and to love one another.

12. What commandment did God give Adam and Eve?
    God commanded them not to eat from the tree in the center of the Garden of Eden.

13. Did Adam and Eve obey God?
    Adam and Eve disobeyed God and broke His commandment.

14. **What is the sin of Adam and Eve called?**
    The sin of Adam and Eve is called original sin.

15. What happened to Adam and Eve because of their sin?
    Because of their sin, they lost their friendship with God and became filled with fear and guilt. They lost their special friendship with each other, and they lost their home in the Garden of Eden.

16. What does original sin mean for us?
    Original sin means that it is not easy for us to trust in God, and we need to work very hard not to be selfish.

17. What did God promise to do after Adam and Eve sinned?
    God promised to send a Savior.

Lesson 3

God Makes a Covenant

Once upon a time, in the land of Ur, there was a man named Abram. Abram was a rich man and he had many nice things, but he and his wife had no children. Even though they wanted children more than anything else in the world, God had not blessed their marriage with fertility.

One day God spoke to Abram. He promised Abram that if he obeyed God, God would give him many descendants, which means many grandchildren and great-grandchildren. God told Abram that he would have so many descendants that they would be a great nation. His descendants would be like the stars of the sky or the sand on the seashore, and no one would be able to count them all. In order to receive this great blessing, God asked Abram to leave the land of Ur and to take his wife and go to a new place far away. Abram obeyed because he had faith that what God had promised would come true. God gave Abram a new name, calling him Abraham. His new name meant that he would have a new life because God's blessing would change his life completely.

God made a covenant with Abraham. A *covenant* is a special bond between two people that neither person is allowed to break. There were two parties in this covenant: Abraham and God Himself. Being part of a covenant is like being members of the same family, and a covenant with God lasts forever and ever.

Abraham was happy to be part of a covenant with God, but he still did not have any children, and he and his wife were becoming older and older. Instead of losing hope, Abraham continued to have faith in God, and that is why we call Abraham our father in faith. After he had obeyed God for many years, God visited Abraham and his wife Sarah and gave them the blessing of fertility. They had a little boy named Isaac, which was a very great miracle because they were too old to have children. When they were able to hold their own son, Abraham and Sarah knew for certain that they had followed the true God, who has power to do anything He chooses, and that all God's promises come true.

When Isaac grew up, he married a woman named Rebekah. Isaac and Rebekah had twin boys. The older boy was named Esau, and the younger boy was named Jacob. Even though they were twins, they were very different. God chose Jacob, the younger son, to continue the covenant He had made with Abraham. God revealed Himself to Jacob and gave him the name Israel, and blessed him with fertility. Israel had a very large family, and his family was called the people of Israel.

After a while, a famine came to the land where they were living. A famine is a time when there is no food to eat. The people of Israel were all very hungry and they did not know what to do, but God had already made a plan to help them. One of Israel's sons, named Joseph, had become an important person in the land of Egypt. Joseph worked for Pharaoh, who was the ruler of Egypt. The people of Israel were able to move to Egypt, where they found food and water and land to live on. Soon they grew into a large nation, just as God had promised Abraham.

The people of Israel were not happy in Egypt, however, because the Egyptians had made them into slaves. *Slavery* means that they were owned by the Egyptians, and they had to do all the hard and dirty work. Even though they were not paid, they could not stop working because the Egyptians would beat them with whips if they stopped. God saw that the people of Israel were suffering and He decided to set them free because He remembered the promises He had made to Abraham.

God chose one of the people of Israel, a man named Moses, who had run away from Egypt and was living in the desert. One day, Moses saw a bush that was on fire but it was not burned up. He went over to look at the burning bush, and God spoke to Moses out of the bush. He told him to take off his sandals because he was standing on holy ground. After Moses took off his sandals, God told him that He was the God of Abraham, the God of Isaac, and the God of Jacob, and He had seen the sufferings of the people of Israel and had come to set them free. God also told Moses His name: "I am who I am." God told Moses that he could say to the people of Israel, "I am has sent me to you." God gave Moses a mission to go to Pharaoh and to tell him that God wanted the people of Israel to go free.

Moses was afraid, but he obeyed God, and he went to Pharaoh with his brother Aaron. They announced God's message, but Pharaoh refused to listen. Pharaoh did not want the slaves to leave because they did all the hard and dirty work for the Egyptians. Pharaoh was also afraid of the people because they had many children and were becoming a great nation. God gave Moses and Aaron the power to work miracles and to cause plagues and disasters, like hail falling from the sky. God caused nine different plagues, but Pharaoh was very stubborn, and he kept saying "No."

God said that He would send one more plague and after that Pharaoh would let the people go. God told the people to gather for a meal called the *Passover*. Each family sacrificed a lamb and marked their house with its blood, and in the evening they ate the Passover meal, which was the meat of the lamb, bitter herbs, and special bread. That night, many people in Egypt died, but the plague passed over every house marked by the blood of the lamb, and the people of Israel were safe.

After this plague, Pharaoh let the people go free. They hurried to pack up their things and leave Egypt, but before they had gone very far, Pharaoh changed his mind! He decided to send the army to kill them. The soldiers had swords and spears, and they rode in chariots pulled by horses. The people of Israel had come to the shore of the Red Sea, but they had no boats to cross the sea. Pharaoh's army was coming behind them, and the people were trapped and became very afraid. Moses prayed to God, and God told him to hold up his staff over the Red Sea. God sent a strong wind that divided the water, and the people walked through the middle of the waters and came safely to the other shore. When the soldiers drove their chariots after the people, the waters flowed back together and the soldiers were drowned in the sea. The people of Israel saw how powerful God is, because God saved them from Pharaoh's army.

God then told Moses to lead the people to a mountain, called Mount Sinai. On that mountain God made a covenant with all the people. There were two parties in this covenant: the people of Israel and God Himself. Being part of a covenant is just like being members of the same family, and a covenant with God lasts forever and ever.

God promised to be their God, to care for them, and to give them a land to live in. The people promised to worship God alone and to keep His commandments. God gave the people these Ten Commandments:

I. I am the Lord thy God; thou shalt not have strange gods before me.
II. Thou shalt not take the name of the Lord thy God in vain.
III. Remember to keep holy the Lord's Day.
IV. Honor thy father and thy mother.
V. Thou shalt not kill.
VI. Thou shalt not commit adultery.
VII. Thou shalt not steal.
VIII. Thou shalt not bear false witness against thy neighbor.
IX. Thou shalt not covet thy neighbor's wife.
X. Thou shalt not covet thy neighbor's goods.

After forty years of wandering in the desert, the people of Israel came to the land that God had promised to give them. The people became a kingdom, and their most famous ruler was King David, who ruled in the city of Jerusalem. After a while, though, the people began to sin against God and break His commandments. They cheated and stole from each other, and they did mean things to each other. Worst of all, they ignored God who loved them very much, and they worshiped strange gods instead.

Although the people of Israel broke their side of the covenant, God did not break His side of the covenant, because God is faithful and a covenant with God lasts forever and ever. God sent prophets to tell the people to repent, and He said that if they did not repent, they would suffer because of their sins. The people ignored the prophets and made fun of them. They continued to sin against God and break the commandments until one day Jerusalem was attacked by the army of Babylon. Some of the people were killed, and many of them were captured and taken away from their home. Then the people learned that even though God is patient, He is also just, and it is very important to obey God.

The prophets had also told the people of Israel something else. The prophets had said that one day God would send a Savior to save His people from their sins. The Savior would make a New

Covenant, a covenant that would be perfect, a covenant that would never be broken. The people knew that all God's promises come true, and so they wondered how God would fulfill His promises and send a Savior.

Lesson 3:
God Makes a Covenant

18. What did God do when he revealed Himself to Abraham?
    God made a covenant with Abraham.

19. What is a covenant?
    A covenant is a special bond between two parties that neither party is allowed to break. Being part of a covenant is like being members of the same family.

20. Who were the two parties in the covenant with Abraham?
    The parties in the covenant were Abraham and God Himself.

21. What did God do for Abraham and Sarah to show that all His promises come true?
    God gave Abraham and Sarah a son named Isaac.

22. Did the covenant with God end when Abraham died?
    The covenant did not end when Abraham died, because God continued the covenant with Isaac and with Jacob, who was given the name Israel.

23. Why did God send Moses?
    God sent Moses because the people of Israel were slaves in Egypt.

24. What did God do for the people of Israel?
    God freed the people of Israel from slavery and made a covenant with them at Mount Sinai.

25. Who were the two parties in the covenant at Mount Sinai?
    The two parties in the covenant at Mount Sinai were the people of Israel and God Himself.

26. What did the people of Israel have to do to keep the covenant of Mount Sinai?
The people of Israel had to worship God alone and keep His commandments.

27. What are God's commandments?
God's commandments are these Ten Commandments:
I. I am the Lord thy God; thou shalt not have strange gods before Me.
II. Thou shalt not take the name of the Lord thy God in vain.
III. Remember to keep holy the Lord's Day.
IV. Honor thy father and thy mother.
V. Thou shalt not kill.
VI. Thou shalt not commit adultery.
VII. Thou shalt not steal.
VIII. Thou shalt not bear false witness against thy neighbor.
IX. Thou shalt not covet thy neighbor's wife.
X. Thou shalt not covet thy neighbor's goods.

28. What did God promise the people of Israel through the prophets?
God promised that He would send a Savior to save His people from their sins and to make a New Covenant that would never be broken.

Lesson 4

God Sends a Savior

After hundreds and hundreds of years, God was ready to send a Savior. The people of Israel had followed God for a long time. Now they knew for certain that God is the only true God, that He is the Lord of all the earth, and that He can do whatever He chooses to do. They also knew that He is patient, and that His love endures forever, and that all God's promises come true. The Bible tells us that it was now the fullness of time, and the world was at peace.

An ancient tradition says that there was a couple in Israel who had no children. Even though they wanted children very much, God had not given them the blessing of fertility. Their names were Joachim and Anne. God had mercy on them, and He blessed them, and a little girl was conceived in Anne's womb. God was present at the moment of conception like He always is, but this time He gave the girl a very special gift. He preserved her from original sin, so that she was friends with God from the first moment of her life. This gift is called the *Immaculate Conception*, and God filled her soul with His grace. When the girl was born, her parents gave thanks to God and named their daughter Mary. Joachim and Anne taught Mary about God. They taught her how God had created the whole world, and how God had made a covenant with Abraham. They told her that the people of Israel had been slaves in Egypt, and God that had called Moses and had set His people free. They taught her the Ten Commandments, and Mary kept all God's commandments and she loved God with all her heart. They also told her that the prophets had promised that one day God would send a Savior who would save His people from their sins.

Mary lived in a town called Nazareth. We give Mary a special name, we call her the *Blessed Virgin Mary*, because God blessed her more than He blessed anyone else. When Mary was a young woman, God sent the angel Gabriel to ask her a question. The angel appeared to Mary and said, "Hail, full of grace, the Lord is with you." Mary was very surprised to see an angel, and she wondered what this greeting meant. Gabriel told her not to be afraid because she had found favor with God, and she would conceive and have a Son, and her Son would be called the Son of God. Gabriel also told her that her Son would be a king and His kingdom would last forever and ever. Mary was puzzled by what the angel said, but she knew that all God's promises come true, and Mary she said to the angel, "Behold, I am the handmaid of the Lord, be it done unto me according to your word." When Mary said "Yes" to the angel, Jesus was conceived in her womb by the power of the Holy Spirit. This is called the *Incarnation*. Mary was the first person to believe that Jesus was the Son of God.

Mary was married to a man named Joseph, but we know that Joseph is not the father of Jesus. The true father of Jesus is God the Father in Heaven. We call Joseph the foster father of Jesus, because he did everything for Jesus that a father does. Jesus was Mary's only child, because she remained a virgin her whole life.

Mary and Joseph left the town of Nazareth to visit Joseph's hometown, which was called Bethlehem. When they arrived in Bethlehem, there was no room for them in the inn. Mary had to give birth to Jesus in a stable and lay Him in a manger. The night He was born, angels appeared to some shepherds near Bethlehem and announced that the Savior had come. Wise men also came with gifts for Jesus. We celebrate His birthday on Christmas day.

Jesus and Mary and Joseph are called the *Holy Family*, and they are a model for every family. Jesus grew up in the town of Nazareth, and He played with other children, He prayed to God, He went to the synagogue on the Sabbath day, and He went to the temple in Jerusalem for the holy days. Jesus listened to the men read the scrolls, and He also learned to read them. The scrolls talked about the wonderful things God had done, and how much God loved the people of Israel. Jesus knew that God was His Father, but it was a secret, so He did not tell anyone.

Jesus lived an ordinary life until He was about thirty years old. One day Jesus went down to the Jordan River because a prophet was preaching there. This prophet was John the Baptist, and he was preaching that the kingdom of God was coming, and it would come very soon. He told everybody to repent from their sins and obey the commandments. People were sorry for their sins, and they asked John to baptize them as a sign that they were going to live a better life.

Jesus went down to the Jordan River so that He could be baptized. When Jesus was baptized, the heavens were opened, the Holy Spirit came down on Him in the form of a dove, and God the Father said, "This is my beloved Son."

Jesus began to preach and teach, telling the people to repent of their sins. Jesus had the power to do signs and miracles to prove that God had sent Him. He healed many people who were sick and cast out unclean spirits that were bothering people. Once there were five thousand men and many women and children who had listened to Jesus preach for so long that they were all hungry. Jesus took five loaves of bread and two fish, blessed them, broke them and gave them to the people to eat. That bread and fish, after it had been blessed, fed everyone, and there was even food left over. Another time, a little girl had just died, and her family was very sad. Jesus took her by the hand and said, "Little girl, get up!" and she came back to life! People were amazed at all the things that Jesus did.

Sometimes Jesus would notice a certain person and He would say, "Follow me." Jesus did not do this to everyone, but only to a few people that He chose. The people Jesus chose became His disciples. A *disciple* is someone who learns from a master by watching him, listening to him, and following him. Many of His disciples realized that Jesus was the Savior God had promised to send.

When Jesus had preached for about three years, He knew that God the Father had one more important thing for Him to do. Some people did not accept Jesus, and they said that He was a bad man, and they wanted to arrest Him. His disciples were afraid that, if Jesus were arrested, He would be killed, because those men were bad people. Jesus knew everything that God the Father had planned for Him, and Jesus loved the Father very much and He obeyed Him completely.

On the night before He died, Jesus celebrated the Passover meal with His disciples. This was the Last Supper, when Jesus gave His disciples the gift of the Eucharist, which is also called Holy Communion. During the meal, Jesus took some bread, blessed it, broke it, and gave it to His disciples saying, "Take this, all of you, and eat of it, for this is my body, which will be given up for you." At the end of the meal, Jesus took a cup of wine, blessed it, and gave it to His disciples saying, "Take this all of you and drink from it. This is the chalice of my blood, the blood of the new and eternal covenant, which will be poured out for you and for many for the forgiveness of sins." This is the New Covenant that Jesus made with God the Father, the covenant that would never be broken. Because of the gift of the Eucharist, every disciple of Jesus is included in this New Covenant. This means that every disciple of Jesus has a special bond with God, like being members of the same family.

That night, Jesus was arrested by the men who did not love God. In the morning, they took Him before the governor and accused Him of saying evil things, and decided that Jesus should die. Jesus had to carry His cross to a hill outside the city of Jerusalem, and there He was crucified. Jesus hung on the cross until He died. He died on the cross to show us God's love for us, to save us from our sins, and to give us eternal life. Because Jesus trusted in God and obeyed Him completely, He overcame the sin of Adam and Eve and all the sins of the world, so that we can become children of God.

After Jesus died, some of His disciples put His body in a tomb, and rolled a stone in front to shut the tomb. This was a very sad time, but the story does not end here. On the third day after He had died, Jesus rose from the dead! This is called the *Resurrection*. Jesus came out of the tomb with a new life that was completely transformed, a life that we call *eternal life*. This means that Jesus will never be hungry or thirsty or tired again, and He will never suffer or die again. Jesus has the power to give eternal life to all His disciples. After He rose from the dead, Jesus showed Himself to His disciples, so that they could see how good God is, and how powerful God is, and so that they would know for certain that all God's promises come true.

After forty days, Jesus took His disciples to the top of a small mountain. He told them that they should wait for the gift that He would send them, and He promised that one day He would come back. Jesus blessed His disciples, and then He ascended into Heaven, going higher and higher and higher until He was hidden by a cloud. The disciples were happy that Jesus was going to God the Father, and they waited in the city of Jerusalem for Jesus to send the gift that He had promised. Ten days later, they received the gift that Jesus had promised, which was the gift of the Holy Spirit. The Holy Spirit came down on them from Heaven, and gave them courage to proclaim to the whole world that Jesus had risen from the dead. The day the Holy Spirit came down is called Pentecost Sunday.

All the disciples of Jesus are still waiting for Him to come back. We know that He will come back again because all God's promises come true. In the meantime, we have the Church and the Bible, and we have the gift of the Eucharist and the other sacraments, and the gift of the Holy Spirit. All these gifts help us to live in God's love and love one another, so that we can truly be the disciples of Jesus.

Lesson 4:
God Sends a Savior

29. *Who is the mother of Jesus?*
The Blessed Virgin Mary is the mother of Jesus.

30. How did God prepare Mary to be the mother of Jesus?
God preserved Mary from original sin at the first moment of her conception; this is called the Immaculate Conception.

31. Why did God send the angel Gabriel to Mary?
God sent the angel Gabriel to ask Mary if she would be the mother of Jesus.

32. What happened when Mary said "Yes" to the angel Gabriel?
When Mary said "Yes", Jesus was conceived in her womb by the power of the Holy Spirit. This is called the Incarnation.

33. *Who is the father of Jesus?*
God the Father in Heaven is the father of Jesus.

34. Did Mary have other children besides Jesus?
Mary did not have other children, she remained a virgin her whole life.

35. Where was Jesus born?
Jesus was born in a stable in Bethlehem. We celebrate His birth on Christmas day.

36. What happened when Jesus was baptized in the Jordan River?
When Jesus was baptized, the heavens were opened, the Holy Spirit came down on Him in the form of a dove, and God the Father said, "This is my beloved Son."

37. What signs did Jesus do to show that God had sent Him?
    Jesus healed the sick, cast out unclean spirits, and worked miracles.

38. What gift did Jesus give to His disciples at the Last Supper?
    At the Last Supper, Jesus gave His disciples the gift of the Eucharist, which is also called Holy Communion.

39. *Why did Jesus die on the cross?*
    Jesus died on the cross to show us God's love for us, to save us from our sins, and to give us eternal life.

40. *What happened on the third day after Jesus died?*
    On the third day after He died, Jesus rose from the dead.

41. What gift did Jesus give His disciples after He ascended into Heaven?
    Jesus gave His disciples the gift of the Holy Spirit. This happened on Pentecost Sunday.

Lesson 5

The Trinity and Jesus Christ

In the first lesson, we said that there is only one God, and that God made everything. We also said that no one made God, because He always has been and He always will be. God is *eternal,* which means that He has no beginning and no end. Even though God created so many different things, He is still greater than all the things that He created. We also say that God is *almighty*, which means that He can do whatever He chooses to do. God is also present in every place, and perfect in every way. We know that God is faithful, and that His love endures forever, and that all God's promises come true.

We have a special name for God; we call God the Blessed Trinity. *Blessed* means that God contains the fullness of every blessing. The word Trinity means that He is one God in three persons. The three persons in God are the Father, the Son, and the Holy Spirit. Jesus Christ is the Son of God, and Jesus showed us that God is the Trinity. When Jesus was baptized in the Jordan River, the heavens were opened, the Holy Spirit came down on Him in the form of a dove, and God the Father said, "This is my beloved Son." At this moment, the three persons in God showed themselves, each in a different way.

We mention the Trinity whenever we make the sign of the cross: "In the name of the Father, and of the Son, and of the Holy Spirit." The priest also mentions the Blessed Trinity in the prayers at Mass, and at the end of some of the prayers he says, "Through our Lord Jesus Christ, your Son, who lives and reigns with you in the unity of the Holy Spirit, one God, forever and ever," and all the people say, "Amen."

Each of the three persons in the Blessed Trinity is God in every way. God the Father is almighty, eternal, present in every place, and perfect in every way. God the Son is almighty, eternal, present in every place, and perfect in every way. God the Holy Spirit is almighty, eternal, present in every place, and perfect in every way.

Each Divine person is perfectly and completely God, but there are not three gods, but only one God. God is a perfect unity, and God is perfect love.

The only difference between the three Divine Persons is their relationship to each other. God the Father is the Father, and God the Son is the Son, and they never trade places. We call God the Father because the Son comes from Him, although the Son is not made and He is not born. Instead, we use the word *begotten*. God the Son is "begotten, not made, consubstantial with the Father." *Consubstantial* means that the Son is God just like the Father is God. He is "God from God, light from light, true God from true God."

The Holy Spirit comes from the Father and the Son, but the Holy Spirit is not made, or born, or begotten, because if He were begotten there would be two sons and there is only one. We say that He *proceeds* from the Father and the Son. God the Father is the Father, and God the Son is the Son, and God the Holy Spirit proceeds from the Father and the Son. Each one is God in every way, but there are not three gods, but only one God.

The Blessed Trinity is united in the deepest, most intense love. Sometimes we say that the Blessed Trinity is a community of love. God made the family so that there would be a community of love on earth, like God is a community of love in Heaven. God also made the Church to be a community of love, and the more we love, the more we become like God.

God shared His Divine love with us when God the Son came down from Heaven. Whenever we recite the *Creed*, we say: "For us men and for our salvation He came down from Heaven, and by the power of the Holy Spirit was incarnate of the Virgin Mary, and became man." This moment, when Jesus began to exist in the womb of Mary, is called the Incarnation. *Incarnation* means that Jesus Christ is true God and true man. It means that the Son of Mary is the Son of God, and the little baby born in Bethlehem is also God. God the Son came down to share our life on earth, so that we can go to share His life in Heaven.

Jesus Christ is God in every way, but He is also a human being in every way like us. He has a body and a soul. When Jesus did not eat He was hungry, and when He did not sleep He was tired, and when someone did something bad to Him it hurt Jesus just like it hurts us. When Jesus had to suffer and die on the cross it hurt Him very much. Jesus chose to die on the cross because it was the very best way to show us God's love for us, to save us from our sins, and to give us eternal life.

We have a special name for the time when Jesus had to suffer and die, and then rise again from the dead. We call this the *Paschal mystery*. We remember the Paschal mystery on Good Friday and Easter Sunday. We also remember the death and resurrection of Jesus every Sunday, because Sunday is the day that Jesus rose from the dead. The Mass is how we celebrate the Paschal Mystery, and through receiving Holy Communion, our lives become part of this great mystery.

God gave us Sunday to remind us of His love for us, and we call this day *the Lord's Day*. Every other day of the week we have to work, but on this day we can relax, because relaxing reminds us that Jesus is in charge of the world and things are going to be okay. We know that Jesus is in charge of the world, because in the Creed we say that Jesus "is seated at the right hand of the Father." This means that God the Father, who sits on the throne of Heaven, has given Jesus Christ all power, glory, honor and kingship. Jesus is the king whose kingdom will never end. This is what we are asking for when we pray the Our Father, and we say, "Thy kingdom come, thy will be done, on earth as it is in Heaven." We want earth to become the kingdom of God, just like Heaven is the kingdom of God. We are disciples of Jesus because His disciples are His servants. When the kingdom of Heaven comes, all the servants of Jesus will be made princes and princesses in His kingdom. The kingdom of Jesus will be more wonderful than any kingdom that has ever existed, and it will last forever and ever. Amen.

Lesson 5:
The Trinity and Jesus Christ

42. ***How many gods are there?***
    There is only one God.

43. Why do we call God the Blessed Trinity?
    We call God the Blessed Trinity because He is one God in three persons.

44. ***Who are the three persons in God?***
    The three persons in God are the Father, the Son, and the Holy Spirit.

5. Why do we say that God is love?
    We say that God is love because the Father, the Son, and the Holy Spirit are united in perfect love.

45. Did God the Father make God the Son?
    God the Son is begotten, not made, consubstantial with the Father. Consubstantial means that He is true God from true God.

46. What did God the Son do for us men and for our salvation?
    For us men and for our salvation He came down from Heaven, and by the power of the Holy Spirit was incarnate of the Virgin Mary, and became man.

47. ***When God the Son became man, what was His name?***
    Jesus Christ.

48. What does Incarnation mean?
    Incarnation means that Jesus Christ is the Son of God and the son of Mary; He is true God and true man.

39. *Why did Jesus die on the cross?*
Jesus died on the cross to show us God's love for us, to save us from our sins, and to give us eternal life.

49. What is the Paschal mystery?
    The Paschal mystery is the suffering, death, and resurrection of Jesus.

50. What does it mean to say that Jesus sits at the right hand of the Father?
    It means that God the Father has given Jesus all power, glory, honor and kingship.

Lesson 6

The Church is the Family of God

God is love, and He created us to live in His love and to love one another. When God made a covenant with the people of Israel, He gave them the Ten Commandments so that they would know how everyone is supposed to live. When Jesus made a New Covenant with God the Father, He gave His disciples a new commandment. The new commandment of Jesus is: "Love one another as I have loved you." Jesus expects all His disciples to love each other in the same way that Jesus loves us. Jesus has loved us by sharing His life with us. First of all, He shared His life when He came down from Heaven and became man. Then Jesus gave His life for us when He died on the cross. This is why a cross or a crucifix is a sign of love, because it reminds us of how much Jesus loves us. Jesus continues to share His life with us through the Church and the sacraments, especially through the Holy Eucharist. Receiving Holy Communion changes our life because we receive Jesus, who loves us and helps us to love one another.

Jesus makes it easier for us to love one another because He makes us part of the New Covenant. The New Covenant gives us a special bond with God and with one another, like being members of the same family. The family of God is called the Church. When we talk about the Church, it is easy to think about the place where we go to Mass on Sunday. There are actually thousands of places like the one we visit, where millions of people are going to Mass every Sunday. All these people make up the family of God which is the Church. The Church also includes the saints in Heaven and the souls in Purgatory, so the family of God is very big.

We become members of the Church when we are baptized. All the members of the Church have the same calling and the same mission, which is to become holy. Being *holy* means loving God above all things, and loving one another. When we love, we become holy like God is holy, and the more we love, the more we grow in holiness.

On Sunday when we recite the Creed, we say four things about the Church: "I believe in one, holy catholic and apostolic Church." These are called the four *marks* of the Church. The Church is one because, even though it is made up of many people in many different places, they are all united in one big family. The Church is holy because Jesus shares His perfect holiness with the Church, through the power of the Holy Spirit. The Church is Catholic because it includes people from every nation of the world and from every situation in life. We also say that the Church is Apostolic. The *Apostles* were the twelve men whom Jesus chose and appointed to be teachers and leaders in the Church. This is a list of the twelve Apostles: Peter, Andrew, James, John, Thomas, James, Philip, Bartholomew, Matthew, Simon, Jude, and Judas Iscariot. The Apostles appointed other men to continue their ministry of being teachers and leaders, and these men are the Pope and the bishops. They are the *successors of the Apostles*, meaning that they teach the same faith that the Apostles taught, and they continue the same work of being shepherds for the Church. This is what makes the Church Apostolic.

The Pope represents Jesus as the head of the Church in the whole world. The bishop represents Jesus as the head of the local Church, which is called the Diocese. Even though there are many bishops in the Church, they are not able to teach all the people themselves, because there are so many Christians. The bishops have men to help them, and these men are the priests. The priests preach and celebrate the sacraments, and some of them are appointed to lead the people who belong to a parish. Jesus works through each one of His priests, and so the priesthood is a sign of His love for us. We should pray for the priests, because their work is not easy, and they need God's grace very much. A priest also needs to go to Confession just like everyone else. A priest cannot hear his own Confession; he has to find another priest to listen to him and to give him the absolution from his sins.

Besides the priests, there are also deacons. Deacons help the priests at Mass and they do other ministries of service. The Pope and the bishops, together with the priests and the deacons, are all called the *clergy*. The other members of the Church are called *lay people* or the *laity*.

All the members of the Church, both the clergy and the laity, are called to become holy. While everyone needs to become holy, Jesus calls His disciples to different forms of life, and these forms of life are called *vocations*. There are two key vocations in the Church: marriage and celibacy. Both of these vocations involve a lifelong commitment, and both are images of Jesus in a special way.

Marriage is a lifelong covenant between a man and a woman, in which they promise faithful love to each other and accept the duty of raising children. The wedding day is the moment when the husband and wife make their lifelong commitment, and the wedding day is also the moment when they receive the sacrament of marriage. The love between a husband and wife should grow and become like the love between Jesus and the Church. Some days it is easy for a husband and wife to love each other, and other days it can be hard. Jesus gives His grace to the couple to help them love each other even when it is difficult. They also receive grace to love their children, if God blesses them with fertility. Parents are called to love their children in a way that reflects God's love, so the family can become a community of love. Even when God has not given a couple any children, they can still become a community of love and share that love with other people. The more each family becomes a community of love, the more the whole world becomes a community of love.

The other key vocation in the Church is celibacy. *Celibacy* means making a commitment not to marry so that you can give your life to Jesus Christ in a special way. Celibacy means leaving everyone in order to follow Jesus and be with Him as His disciple. When a person makes the commitment to celibacy, he or she is making a sacrifice to God. This sacrifice is offered for the whole Church, and so celibacy is also a way of loving our brothers and sisters.

There are different ways to live the vocation of celibacy. One example is the *ordained priesthood*. Ordination means a consecration to God, and Jesus gives some of His power to the priest so that he can serve the people and celebrate the sacraments. The vocation to the priesthood is only for men.

Another form of celibacy is called *consecrated virginity*. A woman who has never been married can offer herself entirely to Jesus, and the bishop receives this offering and consecrates the woman to

God. Through this consecration she becomes a bride of Christ, and Jesus becomes her spouse in a spiritual way. This vocation is only for women.

Religious life is a vocation to celibacy that is open to men and women. Women in religious life are called nuns or sisters. Men in religious life are called monks, friars or brothers. Some religious men are ordained priests, and they can be called fathers. Men live this vocation in a community of brothers, and women live in a community of sisters. Their community might be called a congregation or a religious order. The special characteristic of religious life is the three promises to live chastity, poverty and obedience. Chastity means never having a husband or wife. Poverty means living without many things. Obedience means obeying a person called a superior, who is like a father or mother in the community. By making these three promises a person becomes consecrated to God and dedicated to living the way Jesus lived. Jesus lived in chastity and poverty, and He was obedient to Mary and Joseph and to His Heavenly Father. Since the members of a religious order live the way Jesus did, the order is like a larger version of the Holy Family at Nazareth.

There are also other ways that people can live in service to God. Many Christians live as single people, some live as widowed men or women, and some live different forms of community life. Each of these forms of life can be a way to love and serve God and to have a close bond with Jesus. Just as every person is unique, every member of the Church is called to serve God in a unique way. God loves this variety, and every vocation gives glory to God and is a precious gift to the whole Church.

Lesson 6:
The Church is the Family of God

51. What is the new commandment that Jesus gave His disciples?
The new commandment of Jesus is, "Love one another as I have loved you."

52. What does the New Covenant do for us?
The New Covenant gives us a special bond with God and with one another, like being members of the same family. The family of God is called the Church.

53. How does a person become a member of the Church?
A person becomes a member of the Church by being baptized.

54. What are the four marks of the Church?
The four marks of the Church are One, Holy, Catholic and Apostolic.

55. How is the Catholic Church holy?
Jesus shares His perfect holiness with the Church.

56. What does it mean to say that the Church is Catholic?
Catholic means that the Church includes people from every nation of the world and from every situation in life.

57. What does it mean to say that the Church is Apostolic?
Apostolic means that the Pope and the bishops teach the same faith that the Apostles taught, and continue the same work of being shepherds for the Church.

58. What are the two key vocations in the Church?
The two key vocations are marriage and celibacy.

59. What is the vocation of marriage?
    Marriage is a lifelong covenant between a man and a woman, in which they promise faithful love to each other and accept the duty of raising children.

60. What are three ways of living celibacy?
    Three ways of living celibacy are the ordained priesthood, consecrated virginity, and religious life.

61. What are the three promises made in religious life?
    Chastity, poverty, and obedience.

Lesson 7

The Seven Sacraments

The Church is the family of God, and being part of God's family lets us share in His treasures. God's greatest treasures are the riches of His grace. When we talk about God's *grace*, we mean a sharing in His Divine life, which is His power, holiness, love, and all the virtues. Jesus has given the Church Seven Sacraments to share God's grace with us. The sacraments are signs that help us to know God is present and that He is sharing His grace with us.

The first three sacraments are called the sacraments of initiation. *Initiation* means beginning something, and these sacraments are the beginning of our life as members of the Church. The sacraments of initiation are Baptism, Confirmation, and Holy Eucharist.

Baptism takes away original sin and our personal sins, and makes us children of God and members of the Church. Baptism is the first sacrament, and we need to be baptized before we can receive the other sacraments. Usually Baptism is given to a baby or an infant, because even little babies can receive God's grace and become friends of God. Some people were not baptized as children, and so the sacrament is given to them when they are older. A person receiving Baptism has a sponsor, called a godparent, who promises to help the person live the Catholic faith. Baptism is always celebrated with water, which is usually poured on the person's head while the priest says, "I baptize you in the name of the Father, and of the Son, and of the Holy Spirit." The person is also given a white garment as a symbol of purity, and a candle to represent the light of Christ. At Baptism, a person becomes a house of God and a temple of the Holy Spirit.

Do you remember what happened when Jesus was baptized in the Jordan River? The heavens were opened, the Holy Spirit came down on Him in the form of a dove, and the voice of God the Father said, "This is my beloved Son." Here we see an image for the sacrament of Baptism. This moment is also an image of the sacrament of Confirmation, because the Holy Spirit came down on Jesus in the form of a dove.

The sacrament of Confirmation completes the gift of the Holy Spirit that is first given at Baptism. When a person is confirmed, he or she receives the fullness of the gift of the Holy Spirit that Jesus gave to each of His disciples on Pentecost Sunday. Confirmation is celebrated by anointing the person's forehead with blessed oil, called Sacred Chrism, and by the prayer of the bishop. Usually the bishop celebrates Confirmation, but sometimes a priest can celebrate it.

The third sacrament of initiation is called the Most Blessed Sacrament, or the Holy Eucharist. This is the sacrament that we receive in First Communion. The other two sacraments of initiation can only be received once, but this sacrament can be received every Sunday, and even every day. At the Last Supper, Jesus took bread and blessed it and said, "This is my body, which will be given up for you." Then Jesus took the cup of wine and blessed it and said, "This is the chalice of my blood, the blood of the new and eternal covenant, which will be poured out for you and for many for the forgiveness of sin." At the Mass, the priest says the words of Jesus Christ over the bread and wine. The power of Jesus working through the priest performs the same miracle that happened at the Last Supper. The bread and wine is transformed into the Body and Blood of Christ, but even though it has been transformed, the Eucharist continues to look and taste just like bread and wine. Because the Eucharist still looks like ordinary food, we need to have faith to know that Jesus is present.

The Holy Eucharist is called the Real Presence of Jesus. Because Jesus is God, He is present in every place, but Jesus is present in a special and unique way in the Eucharist, and we call this presence the *Real Presence*. Of all the treasures of God's grace, the Eucharist is our most precious treasure, and we should always receive Holy Communion with reverence. *Reverence* means care and respect for what we are doing. Part of our reverence is that, before receiving Holy Communion, we fast from all food and drink, except for water, for at least one hour, so that we can make space for Jesus. Another part of our reverence is being careful not to drop any piece of Holy Communion on the floor, because each piece has been transformed into the body of Christ. The *Host* is the name for each piece of Holy Communion. All of Jesus, His Body, Blood, Soul and Divinity, is entirely present in each Host, and in each particle of the Host and in each drop of the Most Precious Blood.

Jesus continues to be present in the Hosts that are left after communion, so we put them in the *tabernacle*, and mark it with a burning candle. The candle tells us that the Real Presence of Jesus is there, so whenever we visit the church we can spend time with our Savior. After communion, Jesus is present in a special way within each person who has received the Eucharist so it is a good moment to pray. We have a special word for the kind of prayer that we say when we are in the presence of Jesus who is so holy; we call it adoration. *Adoration* means loving and worshiping God, and this is the kind of prayer that we should say after communion.

Once a person has received Baptism, Confirmation and the Holy Eucharist, that person is a full member of the Church. There are four more sacraments that help us to live the life of faith. Two of these are sacraments of healing: Anointing of the Sick and Confession. Anointing of the Sick is given to anyone who is suffering with serious health problems and to everyone who is close to death. It is also given to people who are old and whose health is not very good. Usually the priest lays his hands on the sick person's head, and anoints the person on the forehead and on the hands with holy oil. This oil is called the Oil of the Sick. The sacrament does not always give healing to the person's body, but it always gives God's grace to the person's soul.

The sacrament of Confession is also called the sacrament of Penance or Reconciliation. This sacrament heals our soul from the sins we have committed, and restores the friendship with Jesus that was wounded by our sins. In the sacrament of Confession, Jesus forgives our sins through the absolution of the priest. In order to receive His forgiveness we need to make a *good Confession,* which means being honest and not hiding anything that we know we did wrong. Before Confession we should make an *examination of conscience*, which is a sincere effort to remember all the sins we have committed since our last good Confession. We also need to be truly sorry for having sinned.

Most people make their first Confession before receiving their First Communion. Sometimes, a person who was not baptized as a baby will receive Baptism and Confirmation, and then receive First

Communion right away without going to Confession first. This person did not need to go to Confession, because the sacrament of Baptism washes away original sin and all the personal sins that a person committed before being baptized.

The other two sacraments are called sacraments of vocation, and these are Marriage and Holy Orders. Marriage is also called the Sacrament of Matrimony. This is the sacrament that a man and woman receive on their wedding day. Marriage is a lifelong covenant between a man and a woman, in which they promise faithful love to each other and accept the duty of raising children. This sacrament gives the husband and the wife the grace they need to be faithful to each other and to care for their children. Even though God intended a marriage to last for a whole lifetime, sometimes a husband and wife separate. This is a sad situation and it can be very painful. We should pray for God to help everyone who is in this situation.

Holy Orders is the sacrament for ministry in the Church. There are three degrees of Holy Orders: deacon, priest, and bishop. A man is first ordained a deacon, and then if he feels called to the priesthood, he can be ordained a priest. Finally, some priests are ordained as bishops. The bishops are the successors of the Apostles, and they continue the same ministry of teaching and leading in the Church. The priests are the helpers of the bishops, and they receive special powers for their ministry. Priests have the power to celebrate Mass, to hear Confessions, and to give the absolution from sins. Priests also celebrate the other sacraments and give blessings. There is one sacrament that only bishops can celebrate, which is the sacrament of Holy Orders. The other sacraments can be celebrated by priests, and the sacrament of Baptism and the sacrament of Marriage can also be celebrated by deacons. Deacons help the priest at Mass and they also do other ministries of service in the Church.

These are the Seven Sacraments: Baptism, Confirmation, Holy Eucharist, Anointing of the Sick, Confession, Matrimony, and Holy Orders. Each sacrament gives God's grace to the members of His Church.

There are also other ways to receive God's grace, called sacramentals. *Sacramentals* are physical signs and rituals that we use to ask for God's blessing. When we make the sign of the cross with holy water or sprinkle it around the house, we are using a sacramental. Wearing a scapular is a special way to receive God's blessing and to entrust ourselves to Mary as her children. We can also wear crosses and medals of saints, and have statues and holy pictures in our house. Lighting a blessed candle is a sacramental. These are all ways of asking for God's blessing and receiving His grace. Our Heavenly Father is very generous, and He wants to bless us and give us His grace, we only need to ask Him.

Lesson 7:
The Seven Sacraments

62. **What are the seven signs that Jesus gave the Church to share God's grace with us?**
    The Seven Sacraments.

63. What are the three sacraments of initiation, which make us full members of the Church?
    The three sacraments of initiation are Baptism, Confirmation, and Holy Eucharist.

64. What are the effects of Baptism?
    Baptism takes away original sin and personal sins, and makes us children of God and members of the Church.

65. What is the effect of Confirmation?
    Confirmation gives us the fullness of the gift of the Holy Spirit that Jesus gave His disciples on Pentecost.

66. **What sacrament do we receive at First Communion?**
    At First Communion we receive the sacrament of the Holy Eucharist.

67. Why is the Holy Eucharist called the Real Presence of Jesus?
    The Holy Eucharist is called the Real Presence of Jesus because it has been transformed into His Body and His Blood.

68. Is Jesus present in each Host and in each drop of the Precious Blood?
    All of Jesus, His Body, Blood, Soul and Divinity, is entirely present in each Host and in each drop of the Precious Blood.

69. What are the two sacraments of healing?
   The two sacraments of healing are Anointing of the Sick and Confession, which is also called Penance or Reconciliation.

70. What does Jesus do in the sacrament of Confession?
   In the sacrament of Confession, Jesus forgives our sins through the absolution of the priest. Confession also heals our soul from the wounds of sin and restores our friendship with God.

71. What is an examination of conscience?
   An examination of conscience is a sincere effort to remember all the sins we have committed since our last good Confession.

72. What are the two sacraments of vocation?
   The two sacraments of vocation are Marriage and Holy Orders.

59. What is the vocation of marriage?
   Marriage is a lifelong covenant between a man and a woman, in which they promise faithful love to each other and accept the duty of raising children.

73. What are the three degrees of the sacrament of Holy Orders?
   The three degrees of Holy Orders are deacon, priest, and bishop.

Lesson 8

Doing Good and Avoiding Evil

God is love, and He created us to live in His love and to love one another. Because Adam and Eve did not trust God and broke His commandment, each person is born with *original sin*. This means that it is not easy for us to trust God, and we have to work very hard to overcome our selfishness. The sacrament of Baptism takes away original sin, and it makes us children of God and members of the Church. Baptism, however, does not take away all the effects of original sin, so we still have to work hard to trust in God and to love one another. Jesus gives us a gift, called *grace*, which helps us to trust in God, to obey His commandments, and to overcome our selfishness.

The more we make good choices to love one another, the more we are able to grow in grace. These good choices form a habit, which makes it easier for us to make good choices. A good habit, that helps us be like Jesus, is called a *virtue*. The opposite of a virtue is a *vice*, which is a bad habit that does not help us to be like Jesus. Kindness is a good example of a virtue. It can be hard to be kind to other people, and especially to people we do not like, but the more we choose to be kind, the more we develop a habit. When being kind becomes a habit, we have the virtue of kindness, and this makes us a kind person. Justice is another example. When we are careful about what is fair for everyone, and not only for ourselves, we can develop the virtue of justice. This makes us a just person. The opposite is also true, which means that the more we take the best for ourselves and ignore other people, the more we develop a bad habit called selfishness. This vice makes us a selfish person. It is important to make good choices because our choices form the kind of person we are.

There are three virtues that we need in order to be friends with God. We call these virtues the *theological virtues* because the word *theo* refers to God. The three theological virtues are faith, hope, and charity, and we cannot live these virtues without the help of God's grace. *Faith* is the virtue of believing that God tells the truth, even when what God says is hard for us to understand. *Hope* is the virtue of trusting in God's promises, even when it seems impossible for them to come true. *Charity* means love, and it is the virtue of loving God with all our heart. The Bible gives us many examples of people who lived these virtues. Abraham and Moses lived in faith and hope. The Blessed Virgin Mary always lived in faith, hope, and charity. For example, when Jesus had to suffer and die, it was hard for Mary to understand, but she never gave up faith and hope in God, and she never stopped loving God. When Jesus rose from the dead, Mary knew for certain that God is very good and that all His promises come true.

Sometimes it is hard for us to trust God because we cannot see that He is telling the truth. It is important to keep trusting God because doubting Him can cause bad things to happen. Original sin is the first bad thing that happened because people did not trust in God. God had given Adam and Eve one commandment: He told them not to eat from the tree in the center of the garden. Eve saw that the fruit looked good to eat, and the serpent told her that if she ate from the tree she would know good and evil. Adam and Eve could have asked God about evil, but instead of trusting God, who had made them and given them every good thing, they listened to the serpent who had never done anything for them. When Adam and Eve ate the fruit, they broke God's commandment, and they rejected His love and His care for them. Adam and Eve were sorry for their sin, but this did not change the fact that they had broken their friendship with God and allowed evil into the world.

When we break God's commandments, we do not allow Him to be the king, and we try to put ourselves in charge instead of God. We also reject God's love and His care for us, and any choice to reject God's love is a sin. Any choice not to love another person is also a sin. This is because every person is made in the image and likeness of God, so every person is special and needs to be treated with love. If we treat a person in any other way, we are not respecting them, and this means not respecting God who created them.

The sin of Adam and Eve is called *original sin*. The sins that we commit ourselves are called *personal sin*. There are two kinds of personal sin: *mortal sin* and *venial sin*. Mortal sins are serious sins, and they break our friendship with Jesus. Worshiping strange gods and many sins against the fifth and sixth commandments are mortal sins, whenever a person committed that sin knowing it was wrong and choosing it on purpose.

If a person has committed a mortal sin, he is no longer living in the state of grace, which means that he is not friends with God. In order to become friends with God again, this person needs to go to Confession. In the sacrament of Confession, Jesus forgives our sins through the absolution of the priest, if we make a good Confession and are truly sorry for having sinned. If a person went to Confession, but did not confess a mortal sin on purpose, then he has not made a good Confession and he did not receive God's forgiveness. If he accidentally forgot to mention a mortal sin, but was truly sorry for it, that sin was forgiven by Jesus but he needs to confess it the next time he goes to Confession.

Venial sins hurt our friendship with Jesus but they do not break it. When we have committed a venial sin, we do not have to go to Confession right away, but we should not wait too long to go so we do not forget our sins or start a bad habit. If you forget to confess a venial sin, that sin was still forgiven by Jesus and you do not need to mention it again. It is important to confess our venial sins because the sacrament heals our soul from the sins we have committed, and it restores the friendship with God that was wounded by our sins. Confession also gives us grace to avoid sins in the future.

If you do something bad by accident then it is not a sin. For example, you might accidentally break someone's toy, which is a bad thing, but it is not a sin if it was not on purpose. Something is also not a sin if you did not know that it was bad. For example, if a friend told you that something was okay with her mother but it was really not okay, it was not a sin because you did not know any better. If you have friends who are always trying to get you to do bad things, then it is better to stop spending time with them. This is called avoiding occasions of sin. *Occasions of sin* are places or people that will tempt you to sin.

Confession gives us grace to avoid sin, but there are many temptations and God does not take all the temptations away. God does not take them away because He wants us to learn how to reject what is bad and choose what is good. Even the saints had to keep making good choices and going to Confession for their sins until the end of their lives. Jesus wants His friends to be true friends. When we have learned how to walk with Jesus and avoid evil, even when it is not easy, then we have become true friends of Jesus.

Lesson 8:
Doing Good and Avoiding Evil

11. **Why did God make us?**
    God is love, and He made us to live in His love and to love one another.

74. What do we call the help that God gives us to do good and avoid evil?
    Grace.

75. What is a virtue?
    A virtue is a good habit that makes us more like Jesus.

76. What is a vice?
    A vice is a bad habit that does not make us like Jesus.

77. **What are the three theological virtues?**
    Faith, Hope, and Charity.

78. What do we call a choice to reject God's love?
    Sin.

79. What do we call a choice not to love other people?
    Sin.

14. **What is the sin of Adam and Eve called?**
    The sin of Adam and Eve is called original sin.

80. Is there another kind of sin besides original sin?
    There is also personal sin, which are the sins that we commit ourselves.

81. What are the two kinds of personal sin?
    Mortal sin and venial sin.

82. What is the difference between mortal sin and venial sin?
A mortal sin is a serious sin that breaks our friendship with Jesus. A venial sin hurts our friendship with Jesus but does not break it.

83. **What should we do when we have sinned?**
We should go to Confession.

70. What does Jesus do in the sacrament of Confession?
In the sacrament of Confession, Jesus forgives our sins through the absolution of the priest. Confession also heals our soul from the wounds of sin and restores our friendship with Jesus.

Lesson 9

Prayer is Being with God

During His life on earth, Jesus Christ was constantly united to God the Father through prayer. Jesus taught His disciples how to pray the *Our Father*, which is also called the Lord's Prayer, so that all His disciples would be able to pray.

Prayer means being with God, and prayer is the most important work that the Church does. Prayer is *adoration* of God who is all holy, and *praise* of God who is great and who does great things. An important part of prayer is *thanksgiving* for all the good things that God has done for us. Prayer is called *petition* when we ask for the things we need. One of the most important petitions is asking God to forgive our sins. Prayer is called *intercession* when we ask God to bless other people and to give them the things they need. We should remember to pray for other people because intercession is a way of loving them. We can also ask other people to intercede for us, especially Mary and the saints, because they are close to God.

The public prayer of the Catholic Church is called the *liturgy*. The liturgy is one great prayer of praise and thanksgiving to God. The highest form of liturgy is the celebration of the Mass, and at the Mass we participate in the sacrifice of Jesus. The Mass gives life and hope to the entire world. The whole Church prays at Mass, and when the people say *amen*, they join their voices to the prayer that the priest just prayed, so his prayer becomes their prayer.

On Sunday, the day that Jesus rose from the dead, the whole Church is called to gather and celebrate the Mass and to join in one great prayer that rises up to God from the whole world. Every Catholic has an obligation to go to Mass on Sunday, unless they are sick or too far from a church to be able to go. There are also other days during the year, like Christmas day, which are called Holy Days of Obligation. Catholics have an obligation to go to Mass on those days too.

The Church also prays through the private prayers of each

and every Christian. There are two basic forms of prayer, called vocal prayer and mental prayer. *Vocal prayer* is any time that we use our voice to pray. We say vocal prayer at Mass and when we pray together as a family or say the grace before the meal. There are lots of other prayers that we can say. The Our Father is the prayer that Jesus taught His disciples, and the Hail Mary is a wonderful prayer to Our Blessed Mother. When we say the Hail Mary, we place ourselves close to Mary as she is praying to God, so that we can join in her prayer and so we can ask her to pray for us. The Rosary is a wonderful prayer to say alone or with other people, and each Rosary is like a journey through the life of Jesus. We can also read the Bible and meditate on the stories in a spirit of prayer. One of the books of the Bible, called the Psalms, is made up entirely of prayers to God. There are 150 psalms to choose from, so we can pray for a long time without using them up. Priests and sisters and brothers use the psalms to pray every day in the morning, in the evening, and at night. This prayer is a part of the liturgy call the *Liturgy of the Hours*.

Mental prayer is being with God in the silence of our hearts. Mental prayer can be talking to God, like saying the Our Father or the Hail Mary in our minds. Mental prayer can also be meditating on God's mysteries, such as when we think about how great God is or about how Jesus suffered, or when we read from the Bible and reflect on what we have read. This kind of prayer is called *meditation*. There is a special form of prayer which happens when our soul is able to be very still, and we enjoy communion with God in the depths of our heart. This form of prayer is called *contemplation*. The most important thing about prayer is that we are spending time with God. Even when we do not know what to say, we can just sit with God for a while, and this is very pleasing to God because He loves us and He wants us to spend time with Him.

We can pray at any time during the day or night. It is especially good to pray when we get up in the morning so that we can offer our day to God and ask for His help. This prayer is called the *morning offering*. During the day we can ask God for help whenever we need anything, and ask God to bless the people that we meet. We should thank God for our food before we eat it, because it is a gift from Him. It is also good to pray before we go to bed at night, to ask forgiveness for our mistakes and to thank God for the good things that happened during the day.

We know that God is present in every place and He always hears our prayers. Even if we say our prayers in the secret of our heart, where no one can hear them, God hears them because the Holy Trinity dwells in our hearts. Sometimes we might doubt that God has really heard us, especially when we have been praying very hard for something and nothing has happened. God gives us good things, but He does not always give us what we are asking for.

It can be especially hard to understand when we are sick, or when someone we know is suffering, and we pray for God to take away the suffering and but He does not. Suffering can be a special mission that Jesus gives to some of His friends. Being a friend of Jesus means carrying our own cross like Jesus carried His cross. When we are suffering, it helps to think about the cross of Jesus and to remember that Mary stands near us and prays for us, like she stood near the cross of Jesus. If we accept our sufferings with patience and offer them to God, they become a prayer, and this kind of prayer is very pleasing to God. This was the prayer that Jesus said on the cross to save us from our sins, and so offering our sufferings to God the Father reminds Him of His Son. Since offering our sufferings is a form prayer, we can offer them for other people as a way to intercede for them. We should remember that because Jesus lives in our hearts, He is with us in our sufferings. Our crosses are not so heavy when Jesus helps us carry them. So, whether we are joyful or sad, we always have a reason to be with God in prayer.

Lesson 9:
Prayer is Being with God

84. What prayer did Jesus teach His disciples?
    Jesus taught His disciples the Our Father.

85. What is the public prayer of the Church called?
    The public prayer of the Church is called the liturgy, and the celebration of the Mass is the highest form of liturgy.

86. On what day of the week does the Church gather to worship and thank God?
    The Church gathers every Sunday, because Sunday is the day Jesus rose from the dead.

87. Do Catholics have an obligation to go to Sunday Mass?
    Catholics have an obligation to go to Mass every Sunday and also on the feasts which are called Holy Days of Obligation.

88. **What are the two basic forms of prayer?**
    The two basic forms of prayer are vocal prayer and mental prayer.

89. What is vocal prayer?
    Vocal prayer is any time we use our voice to pray.

90. What is mental prayer?
    Mental prayer is being with God in the silence of our hearts.

91. Why should we pray?
    We should pray because God loves us and He wants us to spend time with Him.

Lesson 10

Mary and the Saints

God is love, and He made us to share His goodness and His love. Because we cannot see God, it is not easy for us to believe that He loves us. God wanted to come and visit us so that we would be able to see how much He loves us. God prepared for His visit by making a covenant with the people of Israel, by giving His law, and by sending the prophets. When everything was ready, God made a home for Himself in the world by creating a little girl filled with His grace. This little girl is the Blessed Virgin Mary. God kept her safe from all stain of original sin at the first moment of her life, so that Mary was always friends with God. We call this gift the *Immaculate Conception*, and we celebrate it every year on December 8th.

When Mary was a young woman, the angel Gabriel came to her to ask her to be the mother of the Savior. Mary said, "Behold, I am the handmaid of the Lord, be it done unto me according to your word." The Blessed Virgin Mary welcomed the Son of God into her womb, and He was conceived by the power of the Holy Spirit. This is called the *Incarnation,* the moment when God became man. God's grace helped Mary to carry Jesus in her womb and to give birth to Him. God's grace also helped her care for Him, to teach Him to walk, and to do all the things that mothers do for their children.

The Blessed Virgin Mary is the Mother of Jesus, and Jesus Christ is God, so we can say that Mary is the *Mother of God*. Being the Mother of God was the most important mission that God ever gave to any of His creatures. In order that Mary would be able to do God's biggest mission, she was given God's biggest gifts and graces. Of all the people that God made, Mary is the purest and the most perfect reflection of God's holiness and His love. When we honor Mary, we are paying honor to God who made her, because all the graces in her life come from God.

Mary accepted God's love and she received all that God gave

her. Mary never committed even the smallest sin, because she lived her whole life in obedience to God and in humility. *Humility* is the virtue of being small and of knowing that all the good things we have are gifts from God. Being humble means not trying to be the center of attention or be important. Mary never tried to be important, she only tried to please God because she loved God very much. Mary called herself God's handmaid, which is a servant girl. Mary only wanted to be a good servant and do whatever God asked. We are very glad that Mary said "Yes" when God asked her to do something very important.

Mary loved Jesus as He lived in her womb, and she loved Him even more when He was born. Jesus loved His mother with a special love, and He was always obedient to her. Jesus saved His mother in the same way that He saved us, by obeying the Father and by offering His life as a perfect sacrifice. Part of Mary's mission was to be near Jesus while He hung on the cross. Mary wanted to be close to her Son, even when He was suffering, because she loved Him very much and because she wanted to obey God. Being near Jesus meant that she had to suffer. Mary did not suffer in her body, but she suffered in her heart and soul the way that only a mother can suffer.

When Jesus was hanging on the cross, He gave His mother a new mission. He looked at Mary, who was standing by the cross with one of His disciples, and He said to her, "Woman, behold, your son!" and then He said to the disciple, "Behold, your mother!" At this moment Jesus gave His mother the mission of being the mother of each one of His disciples. Anyone who is a disciple of Jesus is also a daughter or son of Mary, and that is why we call her *Our Blessed Mother*.

Jesus gave His mother one more special gift. At the end of her life she, was taken up body and soul into Heaven. We call this moment the *Assumption*, and we celebrate it every year on August 15th. Mary was taken up to Heaven so that she could be made the Queen of Heaven, which is her reward for being a humble and faithful servant. From her place in Heaven, Mary continues carrying out her mission to be the mother of each one of the disciples of Jesus.

Mary loves us very much because we are her children. Mary only wants the best for her children, and she constantly prays to

God and asks Him to bless us and give us what we need. Mary's prayer for us is called intercession. We can pray to Mary, but praying to Mary is different than praying to Jesus because Jesus is God. Praying to Mary means accepting her motherly love for us and asking her to stay close to us and to intercede for us. Mary will help us with many things, and most of all she wants to help us say "Yes" to God and become like Jesus. Mary's motherly love is a special expression of God's love for us.

There are many people who have already entered Heaven and who are with God right now; these people are the saints. The *saints* are the friends of Jesus who live with Him in Heaven, and they are also daughters and sons of Mary and members of the Church. The Catholic Church is so big that it includes not only people all over the world but also people in Heaven. Before the saints went to Heaven, they lived on earth just like we do. All the saints followed Jesus, but each saint lived a unique life, because God makes each person special and unique.

Some of the saints lived to be very old: St. Anthony was a hermit in the desert, and when he died he was one hundred and five years old. Other saints were very young: St. Aloysius Gonzaga was a student who died when he was twenty-two years old, and St. Maria Goretti was only eleven when she died.

Each of these saints died in a different way. St. Anthony died from old age, St. Aloysius died from a disease, and St. Maria was killed for the faith. We have a special name for Christians who are killed for the faith, we call them *martyrs*. Martyr is a word that means *witness*, and these saints shed their own blood in order to witness to Jesus. They died because they loved God more than they loved their own life. St. John the Baptist was a martyr, and so were St. Peter and St. Paul and the other Apostles. The only apostle who was not killed for the faith was St. John; he died from old age. St. Lucy and St. Agnes were both consecrated virgins who were martyred for the faith.

Many saints have become heroes of the countries where they lived. When St. Patrick was still a boy he was captured and made a slave in Ireland. He escaped from slavery and went to France, where he was ordained as a priest and then as a bishop. He returned to Ireland and converted the people from worshiping strange gods so that they would follow Jesus.

St. Francis was the son of a successful businessman in Assisi in Italy. He gave up his money to live as a poor beggar for Jesus. In his poverty and humility, St. Francis of Assisi became a living image of Jesus, and he inspired many people to follow God. Some of the people who were inspired by St. Francis became part of a religious family called the Franciscan Order.

St. Joan of Arc was a poor peasant girl who was sent by God to lead the armies of France. She lived very courageously and she died when she was only nineteen years old. Joan of Arc was a martyr for the faith.

Some of the saints were married and had families. St. Bridget of Sweden was the mother of eight children, and one of her daughters is also a saint, St. Catherine of Sweden.

St. Thomas More was a successful lawyer and the father of four children. He had been made a knight, so he was called Sir Thomas More, and he was a good friend of the king of England and an important person in the government. One day, the king decided to leave the Catholic Church, and he wanted Sir Thomas More to leave the Church too. Thomas More said no, and he became a martyr.

Some of the saints were not famous at all during their lifetime. St. Thérèse of Lisieux was a nun in France and a member of the religious family called the Carmelite Order. She died when she was twenty-four years old, and no one except her family and friends had ever heard of her. After she died, the story of her life, called *The Story of a Soul*, became very popular and inspired many people to love God. She was put on the list of saints only twenty-eight years after she died. The Catholic Church keeps an official list of saints, and being put on that list is called being *canonized*.

There are so many saints that it is hard to remember them all. Many people choose a few favorite saints to be their patron saints. *Patron saints* are special helpers and protectors. St. Aloysius Gonzaga is the patron saint of students. St. Lucy is the patron saint of people who have eye problems. St. Maria Goretti is a patron saint for girls. St. Joan of Arc is the patron saint of soldiers and also one of the patron saints of France. St. Patrick is one of the patron saints of Ireland. Many churches are named in honor of a saint, and some cities are named after saints.

The Blessed Virgin Mary is our mother, and the saints are our brothers and sisters, and we are all part of the family of God which is the Church. In the same way that we have pictures of family members in our house, we can also keep pictures and statues of Mary and the saints. Whenever we see a holy picture or a statue, we should remember that Mary and the saints love us, and that we can ask for their help. God wants us to pray to the saints, because the more we talk to them, the more we become friends, and God wants His whole family to know one another and to love one another.

    The saints lived on earth just like we do, but they lived their lives with faith and trust in God. They became saints by obeying God, by accepting their sufferings, and by loving God and one another. The saints are good examples for us, and they also intercede for us. With their help, we can also become saints. If we obey God, accept our sufferings, and love God and one another, we will certainly become friends of Jesus. Jesus brings all His friends to live with Him forever in Heaven.

Lesson 10:
Mary and the Saints

29. *Who is the mother of Jesus?*
The Blessed Virgin Mary is the mother of Jesus.

92. How did God prepare Mary to be the mother of Jesus?
God preserved Mary from original sin at the first moment of her conception. This gift is called the Immaculate Conception.

93. What does Mary do for us?
Mary loves us very much because we are her children. She prays for us and helps us to follow Jesus.

94. *Who are the saints?*
The saints are the friends of Jesus who live with Him in Heaven.

95. Who are the martyrs?
The martyrs are the saints who were killed for their faith in Jesus.

96. Before the saints went to Heaven, where did they live?
They lived on earth just like we do.

97. How do we become saints?
We become saints by obeying God, by accepting our sufferings, and by loving God and one another.

Lesson 11

Angels

In the very first lesson, we talked about how God made the whole world, and the last creature He made was man. Man is the only creature God created that is composed of body and soul, made in the image and likeness of God. God made the human body to be united to the soul. The soul allows us to think, to choose, and to love.

God also created *angels*, who are pure spirits and have no bodies. The angels are able to think, to choose, and to love. Since angels have no bodies, we cannot see them with our eyes or feel them with our fingers, and they do not eat or sleep. Angels are not born; they are created directly by God. God has given the angels great gifts of intelligence, wisdom, holiness, and all the different virtues. Just as each human being is unique, so each angelic being is unique and each angel has gifts that were not given to any other angel. Each angel is loved by God with a special love that is different from the way that God loves anyone else.

Heaven is filled with angels. They love and worship God, and they serve God as His messengers and His instruments. The word *angel* means a messenger. Angels are sent to bring very important messages and to give special missions. Angels can also deliver spiritual gifts that God wants to send to a person. An angel might bring courage to someone who is afraid, or understanding to someone who is confused, or comfort to someone who is sad, or strength to someone who is feeling weak. Angels can bring these gifts without us ever noticing that they were there.

The angels are also God's servants, and they go on important missions and do difficult work for God. Each angel is different, and so God chooses an angel who has the gifts and powers to do the particular job that He has in mind. The Bible tells us the names of three angels: Michael, Gabriel, and Raphael. All three are called Archangels; the word *archangel* means prince-angel or leader-angel.

Some angels have been commanded to watch over us and protect us while we are on earth, and these are called *guardian angels*.

When we make pictures of angels, we usually show them with large wings. The wings tell us that angels can go anywhere God sends them. We cannot see angels, but they sometimes reveal themselves as part of their mission from God. When the angel Gabriel appeared to Mary, she knew right away that he was an angel. An angel also appeared to St. Joseph in a dream. Sometimes angels appear as ordinary people. The Bible tells us that St. Raphael the Archangel went on a mission looking just like an ordinary person. No one realized he was an angel until he told them.

When God created the angels, He gave them the ability to think, to choose and to love. This means that angels had the freedom to love God or to reject Him. Some of them used their freedom to turn against God. They did not want God to be their king, and they tried to put themselves in charge instead of God. It is very sad that they did this, because they became enemies of God and enemies of all the angels who love God. They fought against the good angels but they lost the battle and were thrown out of Heaven. Their sin against God is now final and it cannot be changed, so they will not repent or tell God they are sorry. We call them bad angels, unclean spirits, devils or demons. The prince of demons is called Satan or Lucifer.

The demons are filled with anger and hatred, and they fight very stubbornly against God and against His plan. They also fight against all the friends of God who are the disciples of Jesus. They spread lies to confuse people, like saying that there is no God, or that God does not love us and He wants to hurt us. They try to make bad things look good so we will fall into sin. This is called *temptation*. When we do sin, the demons try to make us afraid to go to Confession. They know that if we confess our sin, we will escape from their trap, because the power of Jesus is greater than any power the demons have.

We should not be afraid of the demons, because they cannot do anything to hurt us as long as we reject their lies and obey God. God sends the guardian angels to help us and protect us. The guardian angels protect us from accidents and dangers, but their most important work is to guide us away from temptations and sins. Guardian angels can inspire us with good thoughts, help us to see the truth, and encourage us when we are feeling weak. The angels can remind us that God loves us and help us to trust in Him. Angels can give us all these thoughts without needing to use words, so we usually do not notice that they have been helping us.

Since angels are able to love, we can be friends with them, and they can be friends with us. We should remember to ask the angels for help and to thank them when they have helped us. The guardian angels are a sign of God's love and His care for us.

Lesson 11:
Angels

98. *What are angels?*
Angels are pure spirits who are able to think, to choose, and to love.

99. Where did angels come from?
Angels were created directly by God.

100. Can we see or touch angels?
Angels do not have bodies, so they cannot be seen or felt, but sometimes they reveal themselves as part of their mission from God.

101. What do angels do?
Angels love and worship God, they serve God as His messengers, and they help people on earth.

102. Do we know the names of any angels?
The Bible tells us the names of three angels: Michael, Gabriel, and Raphael.

103. *What do we call the angels who protect us during our life?*
Guardian angels.

104. Do all the angels serve God?
Some of the angels rebelled against God and became His enemies. They are called bad angels, unclean spirits, or demons.

105. What do the bad angels do?
They spread lies and tempt people to sin.

Lesson 12

The Resurrection and Life Everlasting

Jesus came down from Heaven to show us God's love and to save us from sin. He saved us by dying on the cross, and after He died He was buried in a tomb. Jesus did not stay in the tomb, because on the third day He rose from the dead. This is the *Resurrection*, and it happened on Easter Sunday. Jesus came out of the tomb with a new life that was completely transformed, a life that we call *eternal life*. This means that Jesus will never be hungry or thirsty or tired again, and He will never suffer or die again. Jesus has promised that He will raise His disciples from the dead and give us eternal life. This is called the *resurrection of the body*.

After Jesus rose from the dead, He ascended into Heaven, and we know that He will come again to judge the living and the dead. This means that Jesus is the one who will judge every person and decide where that person has to go after death.

Heaven is the place that God has prepared for everyone who lives in His love and loves one another. The Bible tells us that there will be no more darkness there, because God will be our light. It also says that there will be no more sickness or sadness or suffering, because God will give us peace and joy. We know that Mary and the angels and saints are already in Heaven with God. From Heaven they can intercede for us and they can send us gifts and graces.

Right now we live *in grace,* which is our way of receiving God's life. *Grace is* a sharing in God's power, holiness, love, and all the virtues. God can increase His grace in our lives when we pray, when we receive the sacraments, especially Holy Communion, and when we do good and avoid evil. The more we do these things, the more we become filled with grace.

The saints used to live *in grace*, and now they live *in glory*, which means that they are completely filled and transformed by God's power, holiness and love. In Heaven, God's glory will not only transform our souls but also our bodies, so we say that we will have a *glorified body*. This means that we will never be hungry or thirsty or tired again, and we will never have to suffer or die again.

The angels are already with God and so are the saints. They pray for us and they help us to obey God, because they want us to join them in Heaven. When someone has died in the state of grace there is a place for that person in Heaven. Many people, however, committed a lot of venial sins or they did not love God very much, and so they are not pure enough for Heaven even though God has made a place for them. Because God is merciful, He has given us a way to be purified after death so we can become ready to enter Heaven. This time of purification is called Purgatory.

We know that Purgatory is painful, but the souls in Purgatory are not sad because they know that God has accepted them and they will be with Him one day in Heaven. The souls in Purgatory are also friends of God and they are members of the Church. You can help these souls by praying for them, and by offering your sufferings for them, and by having Masses said for them. If you know a person who has died, it is good to keep praying for that person to be able to enter Heaven. The souls in Purgatory know when we are praying for them, and they can also pray for us.

Not everyone will be able to go to Heaven, because no bitterness or fighting or evil is allowed in Heaven. Jesus has told us that there is another place after death which is called Hell. When Jesus comes in His glory, He will throw all the demons into Hell so they cannot cause trouble any more. We know that Hell is a place without peace or joy, and it is a place of great suffering, and it lasts forever. The people who reject God's love will have to go to Hell. God is very merciful and He is very patient, but if a person has died in the state of mortal sin, that is, without being sorry for a serious sin he committed, that person has rejected God's love and made himself God's enemy. God's enemies have to go to Hell, because Heaven is God's house, and you cannot enter God's house if you are His enemy. This is why it is very important not to commit any mortal sins, and to go to Confession right away if you have fallen into a serious sin.

Our Blessed Mother wants to help you to become friends with God. You should ask Mary to be your mother, and tell her you want to become like Jesus. We say that Mary has an *Immaculate Heart*, because her love is very pure and not selfish at all. Mary loves each one of her children very much, and even if we have made bad choices and gotten our souls dirty, she still loves us with a very pure love. Mary can help us get cleaned up, and go to Confession, and ask for God's mercy, so that our souls can become pure again. God's love is so much greater than all of our sins, and His heart is always open to receive anyone who comes to Him in humility. Amen.

Lesson 12:
The Resurrection and Life Everlasting

40. *What happened on the third day after Jesus died?*
On the third day after He died, Jesus rose from the dead.

106. Where did Jesus go after He rose from the dead?
After He rose from the dead, Jesus ascended into Heaven.

107. Who will come again in glory to judge the living and the dead?
Jesus Christ.

108. *Where do people go after death?*
After death, people go to Heaven or Hell, or they are purified for Heaven in Purgatory.

109. What is the place where everyone lives in God's love and loves one another?
Heaven.

110. What is the place of purification after death for souls who will enter Heaven?
Purgatory.

111. What is the place where everyone rejects God's love?
Hell.

112. *Will everyone go to Heaven?*
Only the people who accept God's love and love one another will go to Heaven.

Twelve Lessons on the Catholic Faith
Memorization Questions

1. *Where did the world come from?*
   God created the whole world out of nothing.

9. *Who made you?*
   God made me.

11. *Why did God make us?*
    God is love, and He made us to live in His love and to love one another.

42. *How many gods are there?*
    There is only one God.

44. *Who are the three persons in God?*
    The three persons in God are the Father, the Son, and the Holy Spirit.

14. *What is the sin of Adam and Eve called?*
    The sin of Adam and Eve is called original sin.

26. *What did the people of Israel have to do to keep the covenant of Mount Sinai?*
    The people of Israel had to worship God alone and keep His commandments.

47. *When God the Son became man, what was His name?*
    Jesus Christ.

29. *Who is the mother of Jesus?*
    The Blessed Virgin Mary is the mother of Jesus.

33. *Who is the father of Jesus?*
    God the Father in Heaven is the father of Jesus.

51. *What is the new commandment that Jesus gave His disciples?*
The new commandment of Jesus is, "Love one another as I have loved you."

39. *Why did Jesus die on the cross?*
Jesus died on the cross to show us God's love for us, to save us from our sins, and to give us eternal life.

40. *What happened on the third day after Jesus died?*
On the third day after He died, Jesus rose from the dead.

54. *What are the four marks of the Church?*
The four marks of the Church are One, Holy, Catholic and Apostolic.

58. *What are the two key vocations in the Church?*
The two key vocations are marriage and celibacy.

62. *What are the seven signs that Jesus gave the Church to share God's grace with us?*
The Seven Sacraments.

66. *What sacrament do we receive at First Communion?*
At First Communion we receive the sacrament of the Holy Eucharist.

83. *What should we do when we have sinned?*
We should go to Confession.

88. *What are the two basic forms of prayer?*
The two basic forms of prayer are vocal prayer and mental prayer.

94. *Who are the saints?*
The saints are the friends of Jesus who live with Him in Heaven.

98. *What are angels?*
Angels are pure spirits who are able to think, to choose, and to love.

103. *What do we call the angels who protect us during our life?*
Guardian angels.

108. *Where do people go after death?*
After death, people go to Heaven or Hell, or they are purified for Heaven in Purgatory.

112. *Will everyone go to Heaven?*
Only the people who accept God's love and love one another will go to Heaven.